Trouble at the Well

Exodus 2:11-20

by
Dr. Mary Manz Simon

illustrated by
Ron Kauffman

Carson-Dellosa Christian Publishing
Greensboro, North Carolina

Contents

Credits
Author: Dr. Mary Manz Simon
Project Director: Sherrill B. Flora
Editor: Carol Layton
Illustrator: Ron Kauffman
Creative Director: Annette Hollister-Papp
Layout Design: Mark Conrad

Scripture on back cover is quoted from the *International Children's Bible®*, *New Century Version®*, copyright © 1986, 1988, 1999 by Tommy Nelson™, a division of Thomas Nelson, Inc. Nashville, Tennessee 37214. Used by permission.

Printed in Thailand • All rights reserved.   ISBN 0-88724-981-7

Moses had traveled a long way.

"Is that a  beyond the hills?"

well

he wondered.

He needed a drink of ![water] .

water

"Baa, baa," said the  as it passed by.

sheep

CD-2063 *Trouble at the Well*

The ▨ tasted so good.
water

The ▨ soothed his dry throat.
water

Moses untied his 👡 .
sandals

The ▨ soothed his tired feet.
water

Moses found a place out of the .

sun

He closed his 👀 and knelt to pray,

eyes

"Lord, I come on bended knee.
Thank you, God, for helping me."

Then, Moses closed his  again.

eyes

This time he fell asleep.

"Baa, baa," Moses heard.

"Baa, baa," Moses heard again.

Barely opening his , Moses saw

eyes

women at the .

well

" need water, too," he murmured.

Sheep

Then, Moses closed his again.

eyes

Suddenly, Moses awoke.

Angry voices filled the air.

Opening his , Moses saw frightened

eyes

 scatter everywhere.

sheep

Use these stickers on page 15.

Use this Scripture sticker on inside back cover.

Exodus 2:11-20

Men pushed toward the  .

well

The women who cared for the  were shoved away.

sheep

"Stop!" said Moses.

"These women were at the  first.

well

They are caring for the ."

sheep

Grumbling, the men looked at Moses and then stomped off.

Moses told the women, "I will help with the  ."

sheep

Gratefully, the women returned to the  .

well

After Moses watered their flock, the

women left with the  . Once again,

sheep

Moses took a long drink of . He

water

returned to the place out of the . He

sun

closed his and fell asleep.

eyes

Soon, Moses felt a gentle tap.

Opening his , Moses looked up.

eyes

He saw one of the women who cared for

the .

sheep

"Sir," she said kindly, "my father wants you to join us for dinner. He is grateful for your help at the  ."

well

As Moses tightened his  , he prayed,

sandals

"Lord, I come on bended knee.
Thank you, God, for helping me."

Parent and Child Activities

Let's Talk

1. Why did Moses thank God?
2. Why did the father of the shepherdess want to thank Moses?
3. Moses knelt to pray. What do you do when you pray?

Rhyme Time

Finish the sentences to find words that rhyme with  .

sheep

1. You use a 🧹 to:

   broom

2. ▨ comes from a 🪣 that is:

   Water   **well**

3. When the ○ comes up, you go to:

   moon

4. A 👶 can crawl or:

   baby

5. When you smell an 🧅 , you:

   onion

6. A military 🚗 is called a:

   car

7. A 🐥 says:

   chick

Fancy Feet

Moses wore sandals on his feet.
When would you wear these?

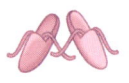

ballet slippers

boots

sneakers

flippers

skis

waders

Sheep Talk!

1. What covers a  ?

sheep

2. Where does a  live?

sheep

3. What is a baby  called?

sheep

4. What does a  eat?

sheep

5. A male  is called a:

sheep

1. wool 2. farm or sheepfold 3. lamb 4. grass 5. ram